WHISPER OF SOUL

NIDHI SHUKLA

ISBN 979-888546061-3

We dedicate this book "Whisper of Soul" to:

The Lord God Almighty Himself

who has ...
carried me,
comforted me,
guided me,
and forgiven me ~
countless times

To all our guides and inspirations, our family and friends who supported and motivated us.

To all poetry lovers and readers without whom creation of this was incomplete.

Thank you all for being part of this book

Contents

Contents

Preface

A collection of romantic, sensuous and steamy poems for all those sensual readers. This book consists of entire range of feminine fantasies and desires. This ultimate bedside companion contains 30 sizziling hot sensual poems that will massage your senses to stimulate and arouse your imagination, mini fantasies and your passion

These poems explore love, lust and intimate relations with personal twist. In the mood for love??? Looking to spice up your boudoir?? Read this or gift this book to your partner to get them hot and bothered before bed, or to inspire with new ideas!!!

Acknowledgements

It Takes Hours To Read A Book But A Months To Write One! During The Inscribing Phase, A Few Writer & Poet Become An Inseparable Part Of the Book. Thancx To All The Peoples For Bring our Strength While I Was Writing this Book.

It Is Every Writer's Dream To Get Published and "Whisper of soul" is One Such Book Of Nidhi Shukla But This Book is more Beautiful by Active Involvement Of Wonderful Scribblings..

Also Thancx To Poetic Souls Publications To Give The Opportunity To publish This Book And For Valuable Guidance And Support.

And Special Thancx To Notoin Press For Providing Such An Amazing Platform For Publishing.

About The Author

A Dreamer,Passionate Lover And A Critique,
Is Masters In computer Applicants And Poet/Storyteller By Passion From Ahmdabad,India.
Her Ink Bleeds With Her Magical Words on Paper.
She Has Co-authored many Anthologies and And Co-Authored 1 International Anthology & compiled More than 8 books.
She has Being Compiling Anthologies As A Compiler And Looking Forward To become A well Known Poet In Future.You Can check Out her Scribblings on Her website: www.rhythmicescape.wordpress.com And on her Instagram Id: @rhythmicescape.She Runs her own Publication House By The Name Of Poetic Souls Publications...

ONE

FANTASY

Yes it is intoxicating but I can't help it out
Just wanna see your body taking shirt out
Lying in the green, early in the morning
I want you deep within deeper then I thought,

I want to be in a swimming pool
naked head to toe,
And you admiring me
and every curve I show....

I want to see you as a cook
with sweat on your chest..
I m on to play along
dirty games in my nest....

Grab from back, close my eyes
pull me close, play with my locks
lock my lips, touch my hips
Strip me slow, come down low,

I want to feel you

down the shower
Where each water drop
raises fire....

I wanna have a candle light dinner
On the seashore
In a dark night
whole body to explore
This is my craziest fantasy, This is my salty desire....

TWO

GAME OF CLUES

Into the lonely island
In beautiful private cruise..
Exploring my body
with the Game of Clues

untie my hair, handle with care.
I need you more.. more to explore..
Feeling high tide.. have nothing to hide
Disrobe one by one, till the game you won..

Nothing more to shy, in your arms I confide..
Lying together beneath the stars
Imprinting my skin and
Soul by love scars..

A cozy morning and the hot tea..
Cuddle and snuggle breaking boundary free
A hot bath tub, where lips you rub
Feeling my skin, moving deep within

Your touch I desire... my feelings on fire..

Slowly setting the pace just right
Taking me to a joy ride
Heard our heartbeat in rhythm, as souls deeply meet..

THREE

NIGHTSTAND

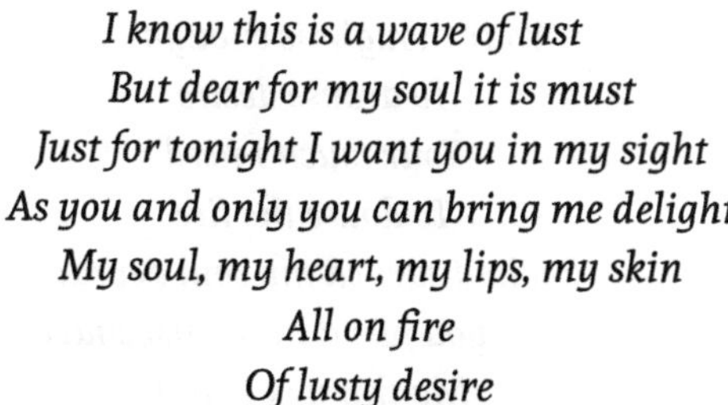

I know this is a wave of lust
But dear for my soul it is must
Just for tonight I want you in my sight
As you and only you can bring me delight
My soul, my heart, my lips, my skin
All on fire
Of lusty desire

I want each inch of your skin
Quenching my thirst deep within
Desire for your touch had grown so strong
I have been craving for you, since so so long
Your lusty tongue on my skin,
You moving it slowly deep within
You saw my face glow..
Ahhh... those nector flow...
The body get closer, While souls get pleasure

And I wish...
Tonight will stay forever and ever
This nightstand I can forget never...

FOUR

DON'T BE NAIVE

Your thought is enough
To arouse desire
Your touch I need
To douse the fire
You had turned my soul deprave
Can't you just a little misbehave
My thirst is rising
Like a high wave
Each bit of skin
Seeking to engrave
Your lips, your skin, your touch
I crave
I want you deep, deep in my cave
With your stare you made me your slave
Hey... now don't behave like a naive...

FIVE

The Tattoo

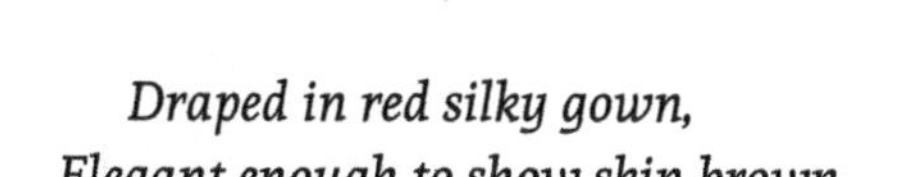

Draped in red silky gown,
Elegant enough to show skin brown
Fragrance of roses didn't make me arouse
It was capitivating stare of yours

Exploring my skin slowly with your finger tips
Each inch of my skin you rubbed your lips
I felt tickling sensation on my nips,
When with force you pressed my hips
Slowly when you unbutton your shirt
Not even a second my attention divert
The tattoo on your musty built
Portrayed you so nicely skilled

Dripping sweat through your chest
Tonight would be a wild quest
This tempting pain only you can cure
Im addicted to flavor of your

I love it all when you bond me tight
Setting the pace the way you like

Gentle and wild we be all night
Not even a moment took off my sight.

SIX

DESIRES DARK

I need you for all my desires dark,
Your touch had just lit the spark..

Your whispers, your breath, your aroma... bewitching
My lips, my skin, my soul is waiting

Stripping my attire with your lips
Grabbing and pressing and sucking my nips
Engraved my skin to mark you win..
But the game has just begin

Pulling my hair you make me moan
Listening which you turned hard as stone

Licking the nectar that just flow
Waiting for me give a blow..
With my tongue I shape that shaft
For a wilder night it was just a draft.

SEVEN

LOST OR WIN

Engraving my soul
Caressing my mole
Lifting me in your arms
Flattering me with your charms

Whispering in my ear
What I longed to hear
Kissing my neck
Finger sliding my back

Ahhhh... you spank my hip
Ouchhhhh.... Don't bite my nip
Through lips we exchange vine
Sould just met like divine..

You turned me onn
All clothes are gone
Pleasure at peak
Your tongue when lick
All juices and nectar flowing
Each moment I feel glowing

I feel butterflies
Reaching high sky
Ahhhh... im so so wet
Just ready to get
My favourite toy
That gives all joy

Every time you move in and out
With pleasure and pain I moan and shout
This night is witness of all the sin..
I just lost it all.. or all I win.

EIGHT

I WANT YOUR MIGHT

For desire of lust
Wild night is must
Like a high tide
Take me to a rough ride
Each inch of my skin
Crave for you
Each moment it creaves more
From morning coffee to evening wine
My heart beats to your rhyme
Addicted to your flavor
Addictied to you aroma
Addicted to your touch
Addicted to your love
Im addicted to you
More than anything in the world
Always I dream
Your lips exploring my skin
And those fingers deep within
Your tongue licking my tight

Wild.. and wilder be my night
Be it wrong or be it right
Only you can bring me delight
Even if its for a night
I want your might
I want your might....

NINE

Hot Shower

In hot Shower I think of you
Each drop sliding over I feel you
From neck to back and down they go..
As if there destination already they know
These drops.. have now ignited fire
Burning my soul in wild desire
Caressing my hair pinching my nips
With fingers I gently pamper my skin
Slowly they found there way deep within
One two and three I go..
Imagining you I tried to flow
With each thrush the fire increase
More for you my desire increase

TEN

Blindfold

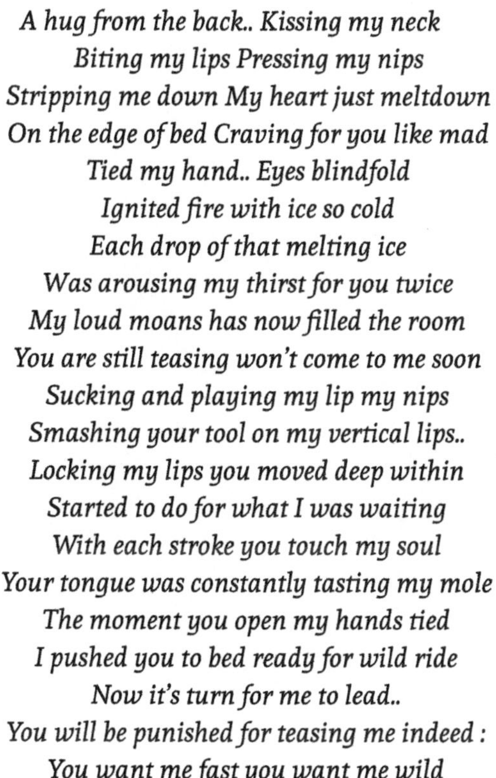

A hug from the back.. Kissing my neck
Biting my lips Pressing my nips
Stripping me down My heart just meltdown
On the edge of bed Craving for you like mad
Tied my hand.. Eyes blindfold
Ignited fire with ice so cold
Each drop of that melting ice
Was arousing my thirst for you twice
My loud moans has now filled the room
You are still teasing won't come to me soon
Sucking and playing my lip my nips
Smashing your tool on my vertical lips..
Locking my lips you moved deep within
Started to do for what I was waiting
With each stroke you touch my soul
Your tongue was constantly tasting my mole
The moment you open my hands tied
I pushed you to bed ready for wild ride
Now it's turn for me to lead..
You will be punished for teasing me indeed :
You want me fast you want me wild

I assure you jaana I wont be mild..

ELEVEN

You Are Mine

I was an ice hard and frozen
With feelings in heart, all shattered and broken
Then one fine day in my life you came
Filled all colors and my heart with your name
You melted me with a hug of you
Love me always the way you do
You are there every time
Every time in my mind
In my mind you are mine...
You are mine forever..
I will let you go never
I will hold you tight
And love you day and night
I will hug you, touch you Fuck you
I will kiss you lick you suck you
You are mine... Yesss you are mine..
Only mine... All the time in my mind
You are mine... Yesss you are mine
I love it all
when you hug me kiss me hold my waist
That passionate kiss

I love it most, I'm addicted to your taste..
When you move in deep you touch my soul..
You make me your slave ready to serve it all
Sweat dripping down chest,
Moving to dream zest..
hands caressing my back. My neck my breast
My vertical lips.. Grabbing my hips
I'm on cloud nine
As you are mine... Yes's jaana you are mine...
Forever in my mind
In my mind all the time you are mine...

TWELVE

DON'T BEGUILE ME

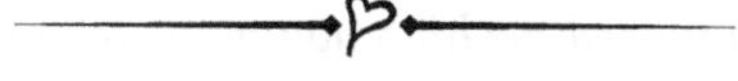

You bewitch me with your smile..
I can feel you even far from a mile..

You hypnotize with your staring eyes
I feel soft shivers and Melting ice

You cast a spell with your charm
I lose myself in your arms

You enchant me with your whispers soft
My heart skips beat as if its tossed..

Your magical touch arouse fire
Makes me high with flowing desires

Your breath on my neck,
fingers caressing my back,

My hand you chained, Eyes blindfold

Your lips your tongue on my skin you rolled..

You enthrall me with your each move
I only obey can not disapprove

You are turning me wild
Don't be gentle and mild..

I want you now deep down inside
Craving for amazing joyride

You turned me high you made me mad
To tease me now... you stood near bed..

I moan I shout your name again and again
You won and made me slave in this game

I need you more from dusk to dawn..
Don't beguile me after turning me on

My hand you chained, Eyes blindfold
Your lips your tongue on my skin you rolled..
I need you more from dusk to dawn..
Don't beguile me after turning me on

THIRTEEN

NIGHT OF PASSION

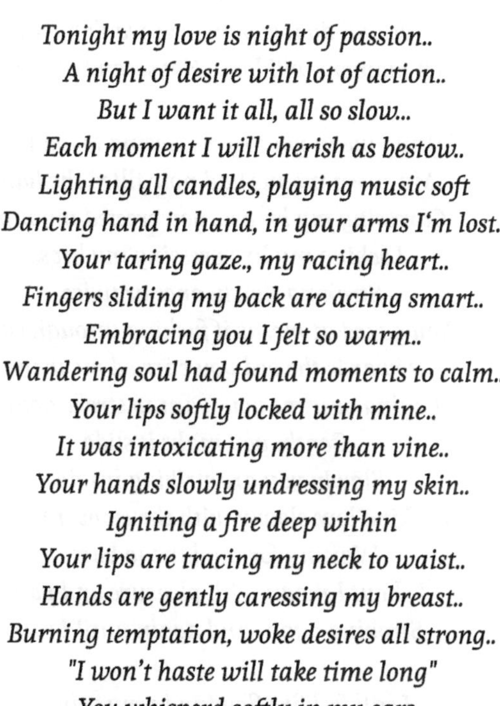

Tonight my love is night of passion..
A night of desire with lot of action..
But I want it all, all so slow...
Each moment I will cherish as bestow..
Lighting all candles, playing music soft
Dancing hand in hand, in your arms I'm lost..
Your taring gaze., my racing heart..
Fingers sliding my back are acting smart..
Embracing you I felt so warm..
Wandering soul had found moments to calm..
Your lips softly locked with mine..
It was intoxicating more than vine..
Your hands slowly undressing my skin..
Igniting a fire deep within
Your lips are tracing my neck to waist..
Hands are gently caressing my breast..
Burning temptation, woke desires all strong..
"I won't haste will take time long"
You whisperd softly in my ears..

Your teasing intentions all I got clear
My fingers moved to remove your shirt..
Your hands were already removing my skirt...
Those tattoos engraved on your skin
I will remake them with my nails deep within
All clothes on ground my heart just pound
Moving to my knees.. Determined to tease..
Scratching your back, spanking your hips..
Taking your hard tool between my lips..
Licking and sucking and playing with your tool..
Choking my mouth you see me dripping and drool..
I'm loving the way my name you moan..
As now my love you are hard as stone..
But...
We will do it slowly... We won't haste..
Each moment will love.. Not second will waste

Lifting me in your arms closing to wall..
My sweet moans had now filled the hall
Caressing my breast.. you erected my nips
Locking my lips pressing my hips..
Stroking slowly once or twice..
You gazed at me, as if fucking through eyes
towards the bed you carried me then
Laying over me you want to stroke again
Gently you make it slide
Slowly you are striking inside..
Making love slowly with thrust over thrust
Waiting for my lava to burst..
I shout I moan with pleasure and pain
Stroking again and again until I rain

I still feel fire flowing in my vein

I plead you to love me again and again
Deeper and deeper you explore me now
You want me to ride you like a cow(girl)
Laying over you I split apart..
Moved you in with a jerk for start..
Slowly setting the right pace..
I can hear your heart beat race
Increasing my speed bit by bit..
Your fingers are rolling and pinching my tit.
My hands are feeling your musty chest..
You spanking me to ride my best..
My name you moan with shivering sound..
Aaahhh..... I'm almost there for my second round..

Slowly passionately we loved all night..
Now sleeping exhausted in close hug tight..
Waiting for the new sun to rise..
What's more to come I fantasize

FOURTEEN

Thinking Of You

Your voice whenever I hear on call
I fondle my skin breaking each protocol
My breath, my beat, so fast they race
With craving moans.. whole body my finger trace.
One hand on cunts.. other playing with nips
Playing with hair I bite my lips
Sucking my thumb I moved fingers in..
Feeling the wetness deep within
Using fingers three my demons evoke...
More wild and deep I want you to stroke
Thinking about you I feel so high
Flowing lava I feel ... between my thigh......

FIFTEEN
ADDICTED

I want you wild, I want you mad..
I want you to dominate me on bed..
I bite your ear, your lips your neck
And then wildly scratched your back..
Whispering in your ear.. In moans unclear
I want you more and more and more
Like a high tide striking the shore..
You got the clue, and made marks blue..
On my neck, my shoulder,
My breast, my waist...
Squeezing, and pressing and
playing with my breast..
Fingers slowly moving down for quest..
I moan, I scream.. I want you deep within..
With closed eyes, between my thigh
I'm melting down with all wild thought
When I feel your wood hard and hot..
Ready to strike on my vertical lips..
Touching delicately with your tips..
Ahhhh Yesssss..
With that thrush you quench my thirst

Movement to and fro... All desires grow
You locked my lips.. To suck my screams..
As you are gonna drive me wilder than my dreams..
Your flavour your aroma your lips your skin...
I m addicted baby to all of yours..
Specially when you are deep within...

SIXTEEN

Close your Eyes

Close your eyes to feel my words
Imagine us in some different world
Lying together cozy and warm
Secured in your arms.. fearless of any harm
Set your imagination on fire
Arouse all wild and wild desire
In the couch on your laps
Softly all my treasures you grab
In kitchen together we cook we lick
Bottomless together closely we stick
In cold shower I found you grown
Filled the atmosphere with satisfying moans
With fingers and dick you are caressing and teasing
Bound, blindfold im begging and craving
Setting the pace of our breath and beats
Wildness and desires even more increase
Again and again with increased intensity
Until you fill me with your fluids velvety
I want to mind fuck you every way
Wild at night wilder in day..

SEVENTEEN

Silky Sheet

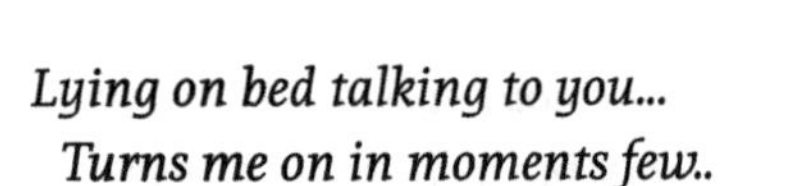

Lying on bed talking to you...
Turns me on in moments few..
Biting my lips.. Sucking my thumb..
Slowly disrobing feelings once numb...

Caressing my breast.. Circling the nips...
All of me is craving... From hair to toe tips
I can't stop my fingers tracing my skin..
Inside my undies... Moving deep within...

Filling my voids with fingers three...
Deep in and out... Even in circular spree..
Aaahhhh... Ahhh... All pleasure moans...
Each inch of skin exploding hormones

Feeling high tide of lusty desire..
Between my thighs can feel flowing fire
Crumbled silky sheet, my messy hair...
Aroma of pheromones I feel everywhere...

EIGHTEEN

Burning Desire

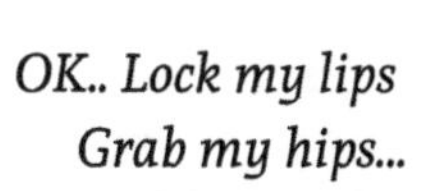

OK.. Lock my lips
Grab my hips...
Hold me tight
Fuck me all night

Deep deep and deeper you go..
Exploring my body the way I don't know
With tongue... With lips.. With fingers you touch..
Burning desires.. I'm craving so much

Shower... Ice.. ignite fire more..
Deep I want you go deeper to the core..
Grabbing and squeezing my melons you moved in..
With such intensity.. That I keep moaning..
Your name again and again..
Pleading to not play any game..

You turned me around.. Groped my breast..
Kissing my neck.. you moved in from back
Placing one hand near vertical lips..
Holdind my hairs spanking my hips

You moved in deeper to make me shout..
And with it our nectar flushed out

NINETEEN

A GAME

Lets play a game tonight
Lay on bed with your hands upright
You can plead, you can moan
But cant bring your hands down
You cant touch me
You cant touch you
No matter whatever I do
Tracing my fingers on your skin
Piercing my nails deep within
Biting your ears, kissing your neck..
Biting your shoulder, scratching your back
I can feel you have turned onn
Between the ham knocking my v.lips down
But..
My love game has just begun
I want each moment filled with passion
From chest to waist your skin I taste
Your breath in my soul taking rest
Ssshhhhh....
You cant break the rule
Else I will skip my riding school

You cal feel whirlpool of testosterone
Even I want to get wrapped in your cologne
Your hands I tied..
Nothing I will hide
Steady and constant you are deep within
Waiting and craving for me to ride
Tying my hairs in loose bun
Thought to play more for fun
Playing and caressing the strawberries
I started to move on blueberry
Feeling the pleasure of your moans
Resting my hand on your chest
Started moving with wild zest
Kissing your lips untied your hand
Playing with my hairs,
Locking my lips
Tracing my back with your fingertips..
Hugging me tight, you came closer
And whispered in my ears
"Now its my turn baby...
You really really teased me bad
For you I was craving like mad
Seeing you with my eyes
All sinful desires rise
Making you blindfold
Keeping your thirst on hold
Laying on the bed
Hands tied overhead
Tracing you with my index finger
To let you feel the love and linger
Finger on your lips
To make you feel eclipse
Licking your neck

Kissing your cheeks
And biting those glossy lips
Pouring your bossom with ice drops
Rolling the finger around your
Kernel desire to make you sweat
Skipping toungue around the
Hard brownies
I want you to crave.. a little more
Coming down to your favourite place
Biting there in your inner ham
Putting ice on your cave
To ignite your lust wave
And when I see your essence drops
I would untie your hands
Pulling you closer from the back
While playing with delicate petals
Giving you the stick to touch
Waiting is now to much
Trying to quench your thirst
Making your moans louder
When you scream with your painful pleasure
To make your nectar out
With the first flow without any doubt
Giving you a soulful hug
Ans whispering in your ears
We travelled our journey
To the paradise which we were craving since long

TWENTY
CUTE DREAMS

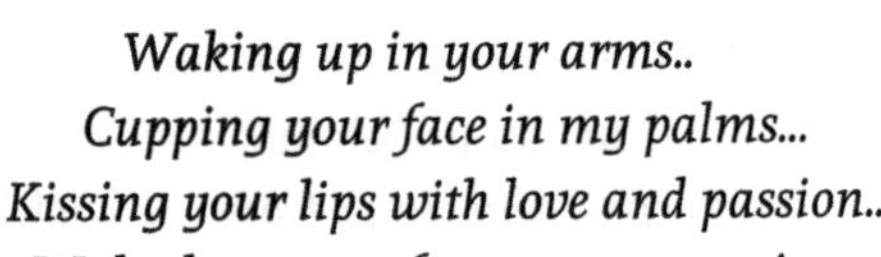

Waking up in your arms..
Cupping your face in my palms...
Kissing your lips with love and passion..
We both are onn for a steamy session..

Lying lazily over you in bath tub..
Squeezing my melons, my Cunt you rub..
Placing your lips over mine..
In my ears you whisper "baby it's now shower time"

Together Playfully cooking our meal
When randomly few kisses you steal..
Hugging from back... your fingers I lick..
Running my hands through your chest to joystick

Romantic candle light dinner with you..
Light music, wine and sweet talks too..
After the dinner a long walk..
Your hands in mine our eyes will talk..

Lying together beneath open sky..

Without wings with joy I fly
Sleeping with my head over your chest..
In our beautiful nest..

TWENTY-ONE

CURE FOR PAIN

Kissing my lips you claimed me yours
You.. only you are cure for my pain for sure
While loving me wild you kissed my mole
Engraved your name on my heart my soul

With each breath you moved deep wihin
In my whispers your name I kept moaning

To drill me deep
In quest of my soul
Pleading and craving
For your love that's all

To quench my thirst
And fill my cave
You... only you can bring
the satisfaction I crave

TWENTY-TWO

LYING ON SAND

Those beautiful night walks With long random talks
Walking hand in hand Lying on sand
And When my love you played your guitar
You took me to the land of stars

Sitting near a bonfire, Heart filled with lusty desire
Beneath the open sky all dreams personify
You took me into your arms
Bringing me all of your charms..

A back hug.. Or a tight snug...
I felt your warmth your breathe your beat..
Kissing my neck caressing my waist..
And with lips lock your love I taste

Beneath the stars u made love scars
Scratching your back biting your ear
I loved you back without any fear
Setting the pace with our heart beat
our souls then finally meet..

Since ages I was waiting for you my love
For ages I wanted to satisfy this thirst

I want you more...
I need you more....
Now I'm an addict
Addicted to your flavor
Your touch your odour
Your talk... those walk
Your love and care
Just be always there
Forever and ever till eternity
Love me always till infinity

TWENTY-THREE

MOMENTS TO ETERNIZE

In that white shirt you looked so smart
Just got blank.. Didn't knew how to start
Holding your hands I then moved out
Without any fear... As you were my scout
Reached a place cozy and warm
Found solace in your arms..
Like high tide meeting the shore...
Again and again..
We were lost in love...
Again and again..
Resting head over you I closed my eyes...
To make this moment eternize..

TWENTY-FOUR

LONG DRIVE

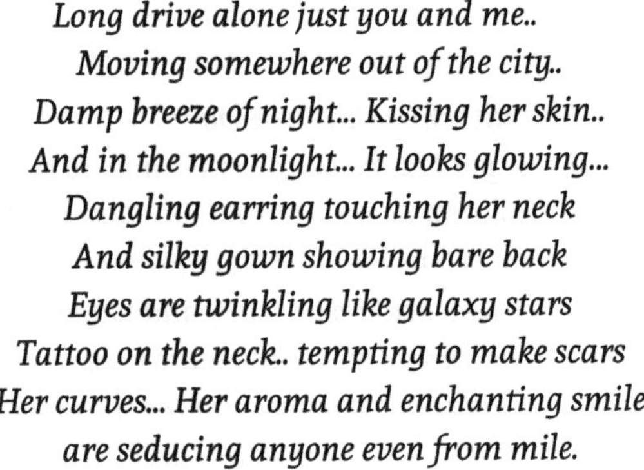

Long drive alone just you and me..
Moving somewhere out of the city..
Damp breeze of night... Kissing her skin..
And in the moonlight... It looks glowing...
Dangling earring touching her neck
And silky gown showing bare back
Eyes are twinkling like galaxy stars
Tattoo on the neck.. tempting to make scars
Her curves... Her aroma and enchanting smile
are seducing anyone even from mile.

Somewhere in dark...He stopped the car..
Looking at me he took the charge
Kissing rose petals, nectar he taste
Caressing those blossoms, he grabbed my waist
Pushing seat back... He made me lie
His fingers traced there way between thighs
Opening his shirt... Kissing his neck...
Hugging him tight.. Scratching his back....
Fingers rolling down

through his chest to his waist
Biting his ears his wildness
I will taste..
Inside his pants I found him hard...
And in my hands I got playcard
Squeezing the balls I made him moan
And with fingers measuring his bone...

Biting her lower lip... I rubbed her clits
To fill those voids.. Her legs I split...
Kissing and licking her soft wet cunt
Making her crave and moan.. Through my tongue
Exploring a little with finger tips...
Swallowing her breath by locking her lips...
Rubbing my lips from naval to waist.
Squeezing those melons erect nips I taste
Feeling her wetness with my bone...
Moving in with a thrush to hear her moan...
Setting the pace of our heart beats.. And breath...
And with love filling her depth
Fading in.. Fading out we found our paradise
Moaning with pleasure.. We closed our eyes

TWENTY-FIVE
WANTING DESIRE

I gaze you with wanting desire
my thoughts get wilder fantasies on fire
Your sparkling eyes..
And that cunning smile..
Staring me constantly for a while..
Hugging me tight you pressed me to the wall
Tying my hands back you made me your thrawl
Sealed my lips...
Groping my hips
Licking my skin from lips to nips
Between my thighs I can feel boner tip...
Pressing my bosoms against your chest
U moved into me with full zest
One thumb near my lips
for me to suck and play..
Other one on my Cunt
Where you would play..
And each moment I moan your name..
To fill me deep and make a claim..
Each touch of you
Made marks blue..

Satisfying pleasure pain..
I feel deep inside too

TWENTY-SIX

SIX.... NINE

By ur teeth my clothes u rip
Caressed my back with ur finger tip
By ur tongue my skin u taste...
Giving me butterflies below my waist
By ur lips I tasted wine..
Biting your neck I marked u mine
Today it's just licking time..
I be ur six... U be my nine..
I felt ur lips kissing inner thighs
It was enough to make me feel high..
Squeezing those petals between ur lips..
And flowing nectar wd tongue u lick
Moving it in.. My depths u explore
Making me crave for
more and more..

With my toy in my mouth
I could barely shout..
But
Could lick it, suck it or give soft bite..

Will take it in deep.. To make u more tight..
Choking my throat
Fluids Drooling my mouth..
Want to taste the honey..
For which i crave
Come for me honey...
And douse this heat wave

TWENTY-SEVEN

UNSEEN.. UNTOUCHED

Kiss my mole..
Satisfy my soul...
Unseen, untouched...
Wd desires to get fucked...
Suck my breast
That pressed ur bare chest...
Beware of wild fire..
I'm burning in desire
Explore my skin...
Hidden treasure within

TWENTY-EIGHT

MOONLIGHT AT ROOFTOP

On the rooftop in his arms...
Still bright moon fails to calm
The fire within him And me..
His sharp eyes ripped all of me...
Just wearing smile on our lips
He explored me with his finger tips..
In the moonlight our skin shine bright
This proximity and heat made us tight...
His breath near my ear...
In whispers my name I hear
One hand on my bossom ...Other running down..
Locking my lips... He sucked my moans..
He touched untouched.. I felt butterflies
He digged in deep.. And crazily I drive..
Our skin got wrapped with all that's wet
Dampness of night, and wetness of sweat..
Here I came.. Tearing apart...
Still he stare.. For another start

TWENTY-NINE

MUSICAL INSTRUMENT

You played me like a musical Instrment
Making me moan on mu high notes
To create melodious symphony
Of rhythm with our breath..

Spanked my butts like coffee we beat...
Aroma of pheromones filled the room..
Like strong coffee just brewed

THIRTY

Whispers of Soul

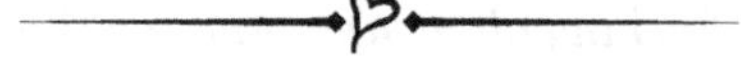

Dream which I had seen always..
That someday we will cross the ways..
The day I will have u in my sight
I will hold ur hands and hug u tight..
Time will freeze then and there
I won't let u go anywhere..
Will talk endlessly whole day
love limitless in all possible way
But...
Seeing u in real.. Can't believe my eyes
Hold ur hand.. To make me realize
Word felt stucked in my heart..
Couldn't even say u looked so smart
Even wd beared.. And cute small tummy..
I stared those lips which looked so yummy..

I felt so peace.. And protected in ur arms..
being sober u were flattering me wd ur charms

My heart was pounding.. Beats were fast
Can't stop hugging you tight at last..
I can feel ur breath near my ears..
Whispering what i longed to hear
Locking my lips.. U quenched my thirst..
Which melted my hearts crust
Ur fingers tracing softly my skin
Gave butterflies deep within
Didn't realized when u moved in deep..
As I was craving for this leap..
U kept my lips locked throughout
Sucking all moans.. And my shout
Again and again and manier times..
We loved breaking all confines
Satisfied my soul.. like an ultimate playboy
u claimed me urs.. Filling me wd joy

About Poetic Souls Community

Poetic Souls is writers community, where we grow together while helping each other.

Motivation and ideas is what we all seek and give. Prompts, Challenges and various activities help a writer to think beyond the box and helps in their overall development.

Apart from this we also provide an author platform which encourages budding writer's to enhance their skills and make their work, reach a target audience of potential readers. ...

Its a growing community of the writers, managed by Rohan Nath and Nidhi Shukla.

9 798885 460613

Printed by Libri Plureos GmbH in Hamburg,
Germany